Esme's Feelings
By Aaron Fields

Copyright © 2025 Aaron Fields. All rights reserved.

Published by The Write Perspective, LLC

All rights reserved. No part of this book shall be reproduced or transmitted in any form or by any means, electronic, mechanical, magnetic, photographic including photocopying, recording or by any information storage and retrieval system, without prior written permission of the publisher. No copyright liability is assumed with respect to the use of the information contained in this book. Even though every precaution has been taken in preparation for this book, the publisher/author assumes no responsibility for errors or omissions. Neither is any liability assumed for any damage that results from the use of the information in this book.

ISBN: 978-1953962-77-5

Theme: Understanding, naming, and validating emotions throughout the day

Esme feels…..a lot.

She feels happy when Papa dances with her in the kitchen.

"You feel so excited," Papa says. "Your joy is jumping!"

Esme feels frustrated when she can't open the box.

Esme older sister kneels down. "You're feeling stuck," she says.

Esme breathes slowly, and Maman helps.

Esme feels curious when she finds a snail outside.

"You're wondering," Papa says. "Snails are slow friends."

Esme feels mad when it's time to stop playing.

"You feel angry," Maman says. "That's okay too."

Esme feels calm after snuggling her bunny.

She feels proud when she helps clean up.

Papa says, "You feel proud! You did something kind."

Esme feels sleepy. Her body is slowing down.

Maman whispers, "No matter what you feel…..you are loved."

🧠 Notes for Adults

Children don't misbehave when they feel---they communicate. Big emotions are not "bad"---they are cues from the brain and body that a child needs something. When caregivers name feelings out loud with calm presence, it helps wire the child's brain for emotional regulation, relational safety, and self-awareness.

This story was designed to model:

- Emotional literacy in everyday life
- Co-regulation through empathy
- Caregiver attunement to facial cues and tone

By slowing down and tuning in to what your child might be feeling, you're doing powerful brain-building work----just by being present.

Feelings change. Love stays.